BOOK I

BENEDICT OF NORCIA

His message today

Anselm Grün, O.S.B.

CONTENTS

BOOK I
BENEDICT OF NORCIA

Part I

Benedict the Man.............................. 05

Part II

The Message of Benedict 13
  1. Living in the presence of God...... 13
  2. Ora et labora - Prayer and work.... 24
  3. Discretio--The gift of discernment. 30
  4. Pax benedicta--Benedictine peace.. 39
  5. Stability and order 47
  6. Benedict's understanding
     of community........................... 53

CONCLUSION............................... 62

ABBREVIATIONS.......................... 65

BOOK II
THE LEGACY OF BENEDICT

The Legacy of Benedict..................... 67

Part I

BENEDICT THE MAN

If after 1500 years one still speaks of a man, indeed, if he is honored with the titles of "Father of the West" and "Patron of Europe," he must have been an extraordinary person. However, if we consult history and try to draw a portrait of Benedict, we are disillusioned. Historical data regarding Benedict's life and activity are hazy; in any case they do not yield sufficient material to construct a clear picture of the man. Again and again the person of Benedict eludes our grasp. We cannot describe him as concretely as we can St. Francis. Yet, it is not the person of Benedict that fascinates us, but his work. He disappears behind his work. He lives in his Rule; through it he continues to work, and to this present day he determines the lives of many monastics worldwide. Benedict fashioned a model of life which in the course of the centuries has been gratefully embraced and experienced, again and again as the means of human development in the following of Christ.

What kind of a man was this that his directives have retained their validity for 1500 years and continue to exert a formative influence on people to this very day? We possess few details of the life of Benedict that can be proven historically. We do, however, know his personality; for through the directives of the Rule, his personality shines forth. From the words of the Rule we gather that he must have been a man of wide experience; a man who recognized the weaknesses and strengths of people from his own observation; who was at one with himself, moderate, capable of leading others, of healing the weak and the sick, of instilling courage and hope; a man, who because he was reconciled with himself, understood how to reconcile people among themselves and how to create an atmosphere of peace about him. And he must have been a man full of faith. For, in the midst of a world in chaos, he was able to confidently, without lamenting the evil times, undertake the creation of a community of monks.

Benedict's life is told quickly. He was born at Norcia in the Sabine Hills around the year 480. As a youth he went to Rome for studies. By then, Rome had lost its importance as the capital of the Empire and showed signs of decay. Repelled by the moral decadence of the city, Benedict discontinued his studies and withdrew into solitude. At first, he joined a group of ascetics at Enfide; but, a short time later he fled from the community and for three years hid in a cave near Subiaco. Here he followed the example of Oriental monasticism: fasting, mortification, prayer, and endurance of attacks by the demons.

"While he was alone, the tempter was with him." Thus, Pope Gregory in Book Two of his *Dialogues* describes this time in the life of Benedict. In his cave the young man was assailed by the storms of passion, fought against them, and came forth victorious. He found the way to peace and harmony within himself. From that time on, he radiated calm and ease. Benedict's victory over the attacks of human frailty enabled him to become a teacher of others. People found their way to him; first among them the shepherds of the locality.

They desired that he announce to them the message of Christ. Later, the monks of a nearby monastery heard of his renown and elected him its superior. But Benedict was too strict for these monks and they decided to poison him in order to rid themselves of him and to allow themselves to continue their religiously tinged bourgeois life. Benedict left and again withdrew "to the wilderness he loved, to live alone with himself in the presence of his heavenly Father" (Dial. 3). "He dwelt by himself," "he returned to himself," "he was with himself"--by these words Gregory indicated an essential attitude of the saint. Benedict was himself; he did not dissipate himself in action. Even in his activity he remained himself, remained whole in it, without allowing it to tear him from his center.

Benedict's breakthrough: becoming a man who was entirely in harmony with himself, did not remain without effect in his surroundings. Unrecruited disciples gathered about him, drawn to him by God himself, as Gregory says. He founded for them twelve monasteries, of which to each he gave an abbot as superior, retaining the general supervision himself. A growing number of Roman nobles brought their sons to Benedict to be educated, which excited the jealousy of a neighboring priest. He had young girls dance before the cells of the monks to tempt them. In order to escape the molestations of the priest, Benedict went to Monte Cassino. Tradition assigns the year 529 as the foundation date of Monte Cassino--the same year in which the pagan school of philosophy in Athens closed its doors. A new school came into being, the school of the Lord. On the hill near Cassino, Benedict established a new monastic community and wrote a Rule for it. The Rule is the most precious treasure Benedict bequeathed to us. From it we perceive his innermost being and how he lived.

Of this oneness of Rule and life Gregory writes in his Dialogues:

> He wrote a Rule for monks that is remarkable for its discretion and clarity of language. Anyone who wishes to know more about his life and character can discover in the Rule what he was like as an abbot; for his life could not have differed from his teaching. (Dial. 36).

For centuries it was believed that Benedict's Rule was an entirely original work. More recent research, however, has shown that Benedict relied heavily on monastic code, above all on the so-called Rule of the Masters. But a comparison with these codes clearly points up the originality and the personal greatness of Benedict.

In contrast to a pessimistic, distrustful and often rigorous view of the human person in the existing legislation, Benedict portrays a trusting attitude toward his monks. This confidence in a person's good kernel was not taken for granted in an epoch when inimical parties outdid themselves in cruelty, when the moral forces of Rome were extinguished and no incentive for fruitful human cooperation surfaced. In this period of lack of confidence, when people lived in fear and mistrust, Benedict dared to believe in the good in individuals and to lead his monks not by undue severity, but by trust, goodness and fraternal love.

By a comparison of the Rule with his predecessors', a portrait of the author can be painted.

Benedict possessed a well-rounded personality. All his directives manifest a wise moderation. He is aware of human weaknesses; he knows that monastics also remain men and women who have to fight the ordinary human problems of strife, dissatisfaction, bad dispositions, dis-comfort, quarreling, dislike of others. Benedict looks these weaknesses in the eye and does not lose his composure in dealing with them. Rather, he accommodates himself to them and heals those who suffer from them. From Benedict's words it becomes apparent that he was not only a realist, but also an optimist who did not allow human weaknesses to lead him to resignation or irony, but who could live comfortably and quietly with deep-seated disposition and strong reliance on God's grace in the midst of human confusion. Benedict did not imagine himself as a leader who performed outstanding feats with his group, but as a physician whose duty it was to heal sick and weak individuals and to make them fit for service in the school of the Lord. For a man to be so equitable and wise, he must have struggled much with himself. The wisdom that appears in the Rule gives an inkling to the experience he himself had made.

Benedict faced the combats and dangers connected with evil; in his quest for inner integrity he looked into the depths of a person's existence so that nothing human was foreign to him. But he also learned of the healing power of grace. And so he became a wise physician who understood how to communicate with people; he did not scare them away by excessive demands, but accepted them in their weakness and so was able to heal them.

Benedict's influence during his lifetime was minimal. He established a community and guided it until his death, probably in 547. Gregory indeed speaks of his preaching to the pagans, of his meeting with the Gothic King Totila, who was so deeply impressed by the Saint that he tempered his cruelty. But we look in vain in his biography for an activity that would merit such titles as "Father of the West" and "Patron of Europe." His influence proceeds from the Rule. His work is more important than his personality. Benedict does not boast of himself and his originality, but in the Rule he points out a way, a way traveled throughout the centuries for uncounted thousands of monks, a way that they found helpful. Still the Rule was never understood solely as a guide for monastics. In the Middle Ages it was a book of instruction for the sons of the nobility and a model for princes. Patently the Rule expresses experiences that are fruitful for the education and guidance of people.

The story of Benedict's activity encourages us to ask what Benedict can tell us today, what his message is for us moderns, not only for monastics, but for all who are seeking God. In this endeavor only some characteristic aspects of his message can be stressed, aspects that appear important for our present situation. In contemplating Benedict, every age emphasizes different viewpoints. At one time stress is laid on his appreciation of manual labor; at another the creative cultural power of the Rule. Or it may be his love for the liturgy, his sense of order, his wise moderation. Every epoch, in its consideration of Benedict, brings forth its own needs and desires to fulfill them. Thus, repeatedly, a subjective image comes into existence. That is entirely legitimate. Still, the images must always conform to the person and to the words of Benedict, lest he be credited with things and ideas that have nothing to do with him. Hence, in what follows, Benedict himself will be the spokesman on the background of the needs that worry us in our quest for spiritual life.

PART II

THE MESSAGE OF BENEDICT

1. Living in the Presence of God

In reading treatises on the piety of our times, the absence of living in the presence of God is lamented time and again. God has become distant to us; we no longer experience his presence in the midst of our lives. There is talk of secularization, of the worldliness of an age in which we are no longer able to meet God. Two responses seem to be available. The first seeks a purely worldly engagement, work in the world: humanitarianism as the proper realm of the Christian; the other stresses withdrawal into oneself: meditation as the way to quiet and silence, as separation from the noise of the world. An attempt to reconcile these two poles appears in the program of the Council of Youth entitled "Struggle and Contemplation." The solution is to let our activity flow from prayer and meditation, and in our activity to be one with ourselves and with God, as Gregory says of Benedict.

Benedict is in a position to teach us a way to a happy synthesis of action and contemplation. He knows of no separation between recollection and engagement, between relationship to God and activity in the world. For that reason we have to keep God in mind everywhere, even in purely worldly matters, including the banal affairs of everyday life. Thus Benedict makes this demand of the cellarer, "Let him regard all the utensils of the monastery and its whole property as if they were the sacred vessels of the altar" (R.31,10). Care of the tools, supervision of property, handling of money-- for Benedict none of this is profane, but has to do with God. In his directive to the cellarer Benedict alludes to the prophecy of Zechariah, "On that day... every pot in Jerusalem and Judah shall be holy to the Lord of hosts" (Zec.14:20f). Hence the cellarer is to regard the property of the monastery as belonging to God. In the management of the goods of this world the monk meets the God of promise, which is initially already present. He need not first separate himself from the world in order to be with God, but while in the world he is also in God, and when dealing with things he is with their creator.

In Chapter 4 St. Benedict indicates what living in God's presence implies, "To know for certain that God sees one everywhere."
In Chapter 7 he describes more clearly what it means to be seen and observed everywhere.

The monk should know:

> "that God is always looking at him from heaven, that his actions are everywhere visible

to the divine eyes and are constantly being reported by the angels." That is what the prophet shows us when he represents God as ever present within our thoughts in the words: 'Searcher of minds and hearts is God' (Ps.7:9).

To live in the presence of God signifies first that I admit him constantly into the innermost recesses of the heart, that I lay open to him all my thoughts and feelings, that I might let him judge to what extent I am attached to myself, how far I am from depending on God. Living in the presence of God is a continuous cleansing process. All feelings and thoughts which arise in my everyday activity, be it at work, be it at prayer, are held up to God's piercing light to be examined by him. Thus, living before God leads to an ever more profound self-knowledge. In the light of God nothing remains hidden--no unresolved problems, no confused feelings, no desires and needs, no thoughts and dispositions. In the presence of God we come into contact with ourselves everywhere. God himself impels us to consider our own reality so that we may recognize it and let it be purified by him.

Living in the presence of God has still another aspect for Benedict. God is present to us as a person speaking to us. The initiative is God's. This is clear from the Prologue in which Benedict says:

Let us open our eyes to the deifying light, let us hear with attentive ears the warning with which the divine voice cries daily to us, "Today if you hear his voice, harden not your hearts." And again, "He who has ears to hear, let him hear what the Spirit says to the Churches." And what does he say? "Come, my children, listen to me; I will teach you the fear of the Lord. Run while you have the light of life, lest darkness of death overtake you." And the Lord, seeking his laborer in the multitude to whom he thus cries out, says again, "Who is the man who will have life, and desires to see good things?" And if, hearing him, you answer, "I am he," God says to you, "If you will have true and everlasting life, keep your tongue from evil and your lips from speaking guile. Turn away from evil and do good, seek after peace and pursue it. And when you have done these things, my eyes shall be upon you and my ears open to your prayers; and before you call upon me, I will say to you, Behold, here I am."

God speaks to us even before we ask him. He employs the words of Scripture. Benedict places the words of Scripture into God's mouth so that they become an entirely personal manner of address. This is no abstract word of God, but a word by which at this moment God speaks to me. The difference in time between God's speech in the Bible and our own life plays no part with Benedict. The words of Scripture are today's words of God, who is present to us.

It behooves us to live with God's word and by his word. Thereby God wants to shed light on the concrete events and difficulties of the day, to make his presence felt in the midst of our everyday existence. If, for example, in a meeting, the emotions and aggressions of the participants hinder a factual discussion, we remind ourselves of the text which Benedict quotes in the Prologue, "Behold, here I am" (Is.58:9): then God himself will be present in the hopelessly confused war of words. He brings a different dimension into the venomous meetings; he changes the situation by allowing us to believe, by the experience of his presence, in another solution, despite the hardheadedness and obstinacy of the participants. God's presence tends to reconcile opposing viewpoints and makes it possible to look at things from a higher plane.

God's presence is not always the same; it is not an impersonal aura that surrounds us, but a person, who ever and again touches us. If we are quietly sitting in our room, we experience God in the passage, "Behold, here I am," differently than when, for example, we remind ourselves of it during a squabble with a fellow-man. Our experience of his presence depends on the situation we are in at the time, and he meets us accordingly in new and unpredictable ways. However, we never experience God simply as an atmosphere of the divine, but always as a person who appears to us with his demands. By his word God seeks to change us, free us of our false attitudes and fill us with the Spirit of the Word.

In Chapter 7, "On Humility," Benedict points out that the inner cleansing process of the monastic is initiated by the word of God. In the twelve degrees of humility he describes the spiritual journey of the monastic. A passage of Scripture governs every stage of the journey. The monastic is to practice what the various degrees demand by contemplating a word of God. Thus, in the second degree one should keep before one's eyes the passage, "it is not to do my own will that I have come down from heaven, but to do the will of him who sent me" (Jn 6:38). And in the sixth degree one should say with regard to all the tasks assigned, "I am brought to nothing and I am without understanding; I have become as a beast of burden before you, and I am always with you" (Ps 73;22f). The word of God does not merely inspire me as to what I am to do; instead it transforms me and produces in me what it says. If, when things are hard and contrary, Benedict has the monastic assert, "in all these things we conquer, through him who has granted us his love" (Rom 8:37; 4th degree), then this word helps him to come to terms with the excessive demand made upon him, not to "crack up" under it, but to overcome it by trust in the Lord and his presence. For Benedict the spiritual life essentially means living in the presence of

God, living on God's word. If I let myself be addressed by the word of God, I will be liberated from my narrow mind and self-love and be filled with God's Spirit. The monastic's asceticism consists in permitting oneself to be transformed by the God who is present and by his word, and in this manner to grow more and more into the love of Christ.

The thought of living in God's presence puts its imprint on Benedict's directive regarding prayer. Because it is God who speaks to us, we first have to open ourselves to his word, we must allow ourselves to be spoken to. This occurs in the reading of his word. Today we run the risk of avoiding God's speaking to us; we think that we must constantly produce prayers, and we fail to note how wordy our prayers are. Or, on the contrary, we withdraw into silence, we flee from the word and think that the enjoyment of silence is already a communing with God. First comes the word of God that addresses me, strikes me, challenges me, wounds and judges me, but also heals and frees me. Both prayer and silence can only be a response to God's word and may not anticipate it. Thus Benedict orders that prayer be frequent, but brief. In it the monastic should respond to God and express his/her readiness to reply to God's word also in action. Hence Benedict gives no instructions regarding mystical prayer, but sobering directives about opening oneself to God again and again in all situations of everyday life. The deciding element is really not our activity, but living with God, in his presence, listening to his word addressed to us and showing us the way. In prayer the monastic replies that he/she has heard God's word and is now ready to follow him.

Living in God's presence, however, does not mean that we must constantly and intellectually be involved with God. That would divide a person interiorly and make excessive demands on him. Rather, it is required that a person open himself to reality, to submit to the all-embracing God. Practice of the presence of God, therefore, does not consist of an exercise in concentration but in letting oneself go, by relaxing and immersing oneself in the reality of God in whom we move and have our being. Hence the practice must be less concerned with the head than with the body.

Our heart should rest in the God who is present. Our gestures, our bodily posture, our manner of speaking, our standing and walking, recollection in all our activity-- everything should witness to the experience of God's presence. Hence Benedict does not hesitate to give definite directives regarding the manner of speaking and bodily postures:

> The eleventh degree of humility is that when a monk speaks he does so gently and without laughter, humbly and seriously in few and sensible words, and that he be not noisy in

speech. It is written, "A wise man is known by the fewness of his words" (R., 7).

The experience of God's presence extends to the voice and bodily posture:

> The twelfth degree of humility is that a monk not only have humility in his heart but also by his very appearance make it always manifest to those who see him. That is to say, whether he is at the "Work of God", in the monastery, in the garden, on the road, in the fields or anywhere else, and whether sitting, walking or standing, he should always have his head bowed and his eyes toward the ground (R.,7).

According to Benedict, living in God's presence puts its imprint on every aspect of human life--prayer, work, the view of creation and relationships with others. "Fellowship," the great slogan of our age does not imply for Benedict any opposition to a pious love of God. The social dimension is already always religious. For in the brother and sister we must meet Christ himself. For Benedict, this is not just an edifying thought, but a reality that affects us again and again in everyday situations. Thus, Benedict says in the chapter on the counsel of the brethren, that all are to be called, "because the Lord often reveals to the younger what is best" (R.,3). Hence for Benedict it is clear that the Lord speaks to us through people, that he can speak through each of us, even through a young person who possibly possesses less experience and knowledge.

Benedict has left us no edifying thoughts regarding meeting Christ in the other person; he takes it for granted. For him it is a self evident reality which ever and again determines his concrete directives. Thus he writes in Chapter 36:

> Before all things and above all things, care must be taken of the sick, so that they will be served as if they were Christ in person; for he himself has said, "I was sick, and you visited me," and "What you did for one of these least ones, you did for me" (R.,36).

The fact that long passages of very sober directives of the Rule are regularly interspersed with such assertions shows that Benedict completely lives in the belief of Christ's presence in the other person. This is a faith that applies not only in extraordinary situations, but a faith that wants to be lived in everyday circumstances, faith that puts its imprint on our daily contacts with one another. That becomes still clearer when Benedict writes about the reception of guests:

> Let all guests who arrive be received like Christ, for he is going to say, "I came as a guest, and you received me" (R.,53).

Indeed the monastics are to bow to the guests or even to prostrate themselves "in adoration of Christ, who indeed is received in their person" (R. 53). If Benedict says that guests are never wanting in the monastery, that their coming is an everyday occurrence, then it becomes clear how faith in the presence of Christ characterizes the entire life of the monastic. Nowadays one may indeed read edifying treatises about this idea, but usually stays only with the edifying thoughts. Benedict, however, regards the presence of Christ in the fellow human being as a reality, in exactly the same way as he sees a brother's load in the kitchen as too heavy. He describes the conduct toward a guest in whom Christ meets us just as soberly as he describes work in the guest kitchen.

Thus Benedict could aid us in being serious about our faith in Christ's presence in the other person, in dealing with others through faith, and in facing interpersonal problems, stresses, antipathies and aggressions on the basis of the reality of Christ in the other person. We feel almost insurmountable barriers rise up within us. And with what an array of reason and logic we then find sufficient ground for asserting that things are not so simple, that distinctions have to be made, and so on! Benedict merely gives the order as if it were the most simple thing in the world. And perhaps this can help us to set aside our rationalizing or our subterfuge, and take seriously the reality of Christ's presence in others so that it will influence our conduct, our attitudes, our words and our viewpoints.

2. Ora et labora - Prayer and work

The combination of prayer and work, the dominance of prayer over work, as Benedict describes the situation in his Rule, brings an important message to our times. Today, many people feel themselves overwhelmed by their work. Everywhere one hears of the stress occasioned by work. Their work seems to alienate them, to burn them out. In opposition to the excessive demands of work, many would like to leave the world of employment. In their quest for an alternate life-style they would not only like to live more simply, but also to work less, sometimes so little that their simplified life-style no longer supports them.

Even groups who are seeking a deeper religious life frequently believe that this can only be accomplished by a reduction of work.

Benedict sees no contradiction between work and prayer. During the winter the monks work five hours and eight hours during the summer, sufficient to earn their sustenance. But more important than a well-balanced juxtaposition of prayer and work is their inner unity. Work should help us to pray well; prayer should aid us in performing work correctly. And finally, work, rightly understood, should become prayer.

Work promotes prayer. In the chapter on manual labor Benedict writes:

> Idleness is the enemy of the soul. Therefore the brethren should be occupied at certain times in manual labor, and again at fixed hours in sacred reading (R. 48).

Work drives out idleness. That does not seem to be a great help for prayer. But it is confirmed by the following experience: In their attempt to live in the presence of God, the monastics find again and again that they would like to flee this reality by withdrawing into an imaginary world. In this imaginary world of fantasy, it is not God, but the person's ego that comes to the fore. Pope Gregory regards it as a sign of pride if one "goes promenading in the vast reaches of one's fantasy by oneself alone" (PL 76. 745A). Since work demands my entire attention and ties my thinking to what I am doing at the moment, it keeps me from flight into the imaginary world of fantasy and helps me to maintain union with God. Doing my work with concentration but without haste, leads me into recollection and by the same token deepens my recollection in prayers.

For Benedict prayer holds the pride of place. Only from the standpoint of prayer can I perform my work in such a way that it has a positive effect on my religious life. Prayer liberates me from work. Many people cannot free themselves from work because they attach too much importance to it. For a long time they continue to mull over it; they worry whether they have done the job correctly, whether perhaps they forgot something. They worry about what others will say, whether the work will be appraised correctly, and so on. This sort of thing cramps us interiorly and overwhelms us.

In prayer, however, we forget about work. We have done our best at work, and now we leave the judgment about it to God. Prayer frees from excessive worry about work. It permits us to live entirely in the present, to concentrate on work, but then also to unshackle us from work, so that it does not entirely enslave us.

Furthermore, prayer clarifies the motives that influence our work. Many problems arise with our work because we have failed to elucidate our motives. A feeling of dissatisfaction, a feeling that we are being burdened and overwhelmed--these are frequently caused by unclarified motives. If in prayer we expose these feelings before God, we will discover what is wrong with us, where we refuse to accept something that God wishes us to do. At times we shall find that we do not wish to accept what God desires of us; rather, we compare ourselves to others and feel neglected instead of doing what God has intended for us.

Benedict lays great stress on the fact that we are to perform our work for pure motives. For him, *motivation* at work is more important than the *result*. Thus he writes in Chapter 57:

If there are craftsmen in the monastery, let them practice their craft with all humility, provided the abbot has given permission. But if one of them becomes conceited over his skill in his craft, because he seems to be conferring a benefit on the monastery, let him be taken from his craft and no longer exercise it unless, after he has humbled himself, the abbot again gives him permission.

Work is, then, only worship of God if I am not unduly attached to it, if I do not abuse it for my own aggrandizement.

For Benedict prayer and work demand the same attitude: humility, readiness to accept God's will and to serve God and not oneself. The criterion for judging whether I serve God or myself by my work is this: Am I ready to undertake some other work if the needs of the com-munity call for it? As Benedict understands it, work demands renunciation of self. Only when it is performed in selfless love does work glorify God just as prayer does.

Co-workers cause us the most difficulty at work. One is slow to grasp things, another gets on our nerves by his or her loquacity. Here prayer can help in reaching a positive relationship with our co-workers. If we pray for them, express thanks for them, then we will create a more humane atmosphere about us and be able to get along better with our fellow human beings.

In the last analysis Benedict considers prayer and work as one, based on his belief in the presence of God. Work becomes prayer when performed in the presence of God; I then respond to God in all of my outward activity; I can dedicate myself entirely to my work without being divided in mind. Immersing myself in work happens in obedience to God and in response to his presence. Here, too, the presence of God places its seal on my manner of working. The person who works carelessly, who wants to do everything at once, regularly loses God's presence. Working in God's presence requires that I perform my task quietly and without haste, recollected in mind and devoting myself entirely to my task.

In Benedict's instructions to the cellarer that he is to treat the tools and property of the monastery as if they were the sacred vessels of the altar, he indicates that in his work the monastic is in constant contact with God. This passage bespeaks the reverence Benedict had for things. Since we find traces of God everywhere in the world, we can only treat the world reverently. In view of the abuse of the environment, we have again become attentive to this message. Already in Benedict's day, a mindless rape of the human environment was committed. The land was devastated by roving bands of outlaws and forests were uprooted for war purposes. The fields lay fallow. The hatred of peoples for one another had also destroyed nature.

Through his monasteries, Benedict created small, self-sufficient economic entities in the midst of a chaotic economic situation. They utilized the basic productivity of the soil, and led to the work of the crafts and to various services. These small entities were not concerned with maximizing profits; their guiding principle was the glory of God. Benedict demanded that his monks sell their products more cheaply than people in the world, "so that in all things God be glorified" (1 Pet. 4:11; R. 57). Neither the quest for monetary gain, nor the plundering of the earth, but reverence for creation and praise of God the Creator were to characterize the work of the monk. He must not despoil the earth, but must treat it in such a way that it reflects the Creator and praises him. It must be our aim, too, to draw the earth into the vision of God. That will only happen if we listen to God's words in creation and reflect on God's purposes regarding the earth. We must understand that not we, but God, has ownership of the world and that we are only its stewards. Creation proclaims its creator and points to the end of time when everything will be the Lord's holy possession.

It appears that Benedict's combination of prayer and work is of decisive importance precisely for our day. We cannot simply withdraw ourselves from the work process. On the other hand, work is more than a necessary evil without which we cannot earn our sustenance. If we join work and prayer, work becomes the site of the spiritual life, a place that does not separate us from God, but in which we can practice the correct attitude toward God: obedience, patience, moderation, trust, selflessness and love. For many, flight from work is at the same time flight from the realities of life and thus flight from God. Benedict could well teach us how to master work by prayer and how to understand it as prayer itself by teaching us to place ourselves and our work before the God who is present, and allowing him to urge us on to fatigue and exhaustion of the body.

3. Discretio - The gift of discernment

Another characteristic of Benedict is his high esteem for discretion, for moderation, for the gift of the discernment of the spirits. At present the religious situation is marked by two extremes--laxism and rigorism. The numerous youth cults, abhorrent accounts of mass murders by fantasized followers of cults have frightened the public. And yet, on the other hand, many embrace rigorous rules and carry them out in practice. Benedict's message is scarcely calculated to call forth waves of enthusiasm. It renounces all excessively high aspirations preferring to deal with people in wise moderation. Holding out lofty ideals always runs the danger of forcing a special identity on the person; this is at the same time an invitation to flee from oneself, since it tends to suppress a person's negative aspects. Young people, in particular those who suffer from an inferiority complex, expect an increase of self esteem by identification with a high ideal.

Benedict does not need to resort to psychological tricks in order to recruit members for his community. He gives a very sober description of his intentions regarding the monastic life:

> And so we are going to establish a school for the service of the Lord. In founding it we hope to introduce nothing harsh or burdensome. But if a certain strictness results from the dictates of equity for the amendment of vices or the preservation of charity, do not be at once dismayed and flee from the way of salvation, whose entrance cannot be but narrow (Prologue).

There is no striving for a lofty ideal or achievement. All the directives, rather, are for the benefit of the person and his salvation. For Benedict, the *person* occupies the center of the stage. One is to be healed; one should find the way to life. The person is not used as a means; one is not subjected to the dictates of a project, not even a religious project. Benedict does not recruit his members with propaganda about impressive works which the monastery will carry out in the service of God or of mankind. For Benedict, such recruiting would stress the external and would subject one to the demands of the project. Benedict wants to treat all persons properly, including the weak. He does not preach a religion of the strong. He rejects the enthusiasm which can be engendered by exaggerated prospects. He reckons with the weakness of men and desires to lead the weak to life as well. This demands a way of wise moderation which measures itself not by self conceived ideals, but by the individual. This is precisely what makes Benedict's teaching a rule of life for many. Benedict does not scare away, he gives courage, he lifts up. Despite his realism, which is aware of all human weaknesses based on his own experience, he remains an optimist. He promises a way of life especially for the weak, the difficult, the average, those wearing themselves out with commonplace problems.

Be it noted, however, that discretion is not an accommodation to the modern life-style, to the modes and maxims of our society. It would be a fatal misreading of Benedict's intentions if we were to interpret discretion as a justification of a bourgeois life-style in the monastery. That kind of monasticism can in no way call on Benedict for support. Instead, Benedict understands discretion as a virtue which orders all things in such a way that the strong are attracted and the weak are not repelled (R.,64). The strong may not simply lower themselves to the level of the weak, rather, they are to be encouraged in their striving, yet so that the weak are not thereby discouraged, but stimulated. The strong must support the weak. For the early monks that was a sign of real strength.

Modern psychology teaches the same lesson: only the person strong enough to accept his own weaknesses can bear with the weak and support them. We are discontented with the weak because they remind us of the weaknesses we have overcome with much effort. We would rather have nothing more to do with them. Benedict encourages the strong in his community to bear with the weak without exalting themselves, but rather understand them because of the knowledge of their own weaknesses and out of gratitude for God's help which is given only on condition that it be handed on to others. Hence, Benedict is not concerned with making fewer demands, but with stimulating both the strong and the weak. Such encouragement prevents a division of the community into "champions" and "lemmings" and unites all in the grace of God by which they know they are borne up.

Discretion, as the gift of discernment, is above all the virtue of the abbot, the virtue of everyone called to lead and guide, educate and form others. So Benedict demands of the abbot:

> In his commands let him be prudent and considerate; and whether the work which he enjoins concerns God or the world, let him be discreet and moderate, bearing in mind

the discretion of holy Jacob who said, "If I cause my flocks to be overdriven, they will all die in one day" (R.,64).

The gift of discernment not only presupposes a correct appreciation of the situation as well as much knowledge and experience, but, above all, a distancing from oneself. Judgment is not to be clouded by the ego, by one's own desires and needs. It must be free of what modern psychology calls projection: unresolved problems, emotions and impulses which a person does not perceive clearly in himself and thus projects onto others. Hence discretion takes for granted that a person has come to know oneself by careful self-observation, that one understands one's needs and is aware of one's emotions and aggressions.

For the monastics, discretion signifies discernment of the spirits. This is a gift that indeed calls for thorough self-observation, but in the final analysis is a gift of God's grace. One must investigate one's own thoughts with regard to the spirit they manifest: Do I let myself be guided by my own spirit or by God's spirit? Whence arise the various desires and impulses? Do they come from God or from the devil? Ultimately, the gift of discernment can be obtained only in prayerful communing with God, in immersing oneself into God's spirit.

Discretion was considered by the monastic as the mother of virtues. Benedict shares this opinion (cf R.,64). It is characteristic of him that he applies it not only to spiritual matters, for example, the spiritual direction of a person, but also to everyday matters. Worldly affairs, too, have something to do with God's Spirit. I must decide whether I will allow myself to be guided also in temporal affairs by the Holy Spirit or by my own spirit. Whether I follow God's Spirit or my own can manifest itself, for example, in the decision for or against the purchase of a machine. Thus, just as I should permeate my work with prayer, so I should always make temporal decisions with reference to God's Spirit. The Spirit will prevent me from letting my emotions and unacknowledged needs influence my decisions. God's Spirit allows me to be objective. He enables me to listen to God's voice in everyday matters.

Discretion is not something arbitrary; it does not justify itself uncontrollably by invoking enlightenment by God's Spirit, but it implies listening to the Spirit who speaks to me through things, through people and through circumstances, who lays bare my own unconscious desires and needs and enables me to recognize God's will in a given situation.

At present many persons have learned anew to listen to God's Spirit. True, at times one gets the impression that a person is confusing caprice with the Spirit of God. Some, in their appeal to the Spirit, lose their footing. In this situation Benedict can show us how prudent we must be in order to possess discretion, the mother of virtues; how sensible we must be while listening at the same time to the Spirit of God, to people and various situations. Human considerations and listening to the Spirit belong together, so that precisely in the discernment of spirits I may be enabled to judge and decide more realistically and humanely. With Benedict, discernment of spirits has nothing out of the ordinary about it. One need only read his advice to the abbot to know that he has his feet firmly on the ground, yet allowing the Spirit of God to shine forth everywhere:

> He should hate vices; he should love the brethren. In administering corrections he should act prudently and not go to excess, lest in seeking too eagerly to scrape off the rust he breaks the vessel. Let him keep his own frailty ever before his eyes and remember that the bruised reed must not be broken. By this we do not mean that he should allow vices to grow; on the contrary, as we have already said, he should eradicate them prudently and with charity, in the way which may seem best in each case. Let him study rather to be loved than to be feared. Let him not be excitable and worried, nor exacting and headstrong, not jealous and over-suspicious, for then he is never at rest (R., 64). The abbot should always remember what he is and what he is called, and should know that those to whom more is committed, from them more is required. Let him understand also what a difficult and arduous task he has undertaken: ruling souls

and adapting himself to a variety of characters. One he must coax, another scold, another persuade, according to each one's character and understanding. Thus he must adjust and adapt himself to all in such a way that he may not only suffer no loss in the flock committed to his care, but may even rejoice in the increase of a good flock (R., 2).

These passages make it abundantly clear that Benedict does not subscribe either to abstract ideals or to sterile principles. He is concerned about the person. The abbot must deal justly with everyone. He should take the individual as he finds him; in every situation he should inquire into the specific will of God. Discretion brings order and clarity into community life, but it rejects sterile rules and principles. For those who have to deal with people it is easier to abide by a set of norms than to consider every individual. But constantly insisting on our rules and barricading ourselves behind principles reveals our fear and uncertainty. Because we are afraid of our own frailty, we hide behind principles without noticing that we are subjecting ourselves and those around us to rules, and as a result, are enslaving ourselves in the process.

Benedict's discretion has nothing to do with sterile principles. Benedict considers the individual, accommodates himself to the needs of everyone. He indeed sets up principles, but constantly disregards them in order to take cognizance of the actual person and the eventual situation. He submits everyone to the wise judgment of the abbot rather than to an absolutely inflexible rule. This manifests great confidence in the judgment of a human being, a judgment capable of knowing clearly and of deciding from his discernment of spirits, of listening to God. The passages bear witness to human frailty and at the same time to the experience of the grace of God, which sustains us in our weakness and enables us to support one another.

Not without reason was the Rule of Benedict for centuries the pedagogical book par excellence. Discretion as the criterion of all education today, might also be more profitable for young people than many of the educational theories based on abstract ideals rather than on real persons. Above all, however, this Benedictine discretion might help us get along with one another as human beings. Today we run the risk of judging the other person according to psychological criteria and wanting to change the person who does not fit those criteria. We no longer notice that we apply our own yardstick to another, thus implying that we know exactly what is normal and good for others. From Benedict we might learn to jettison all the psychological theories that tend to cloud the opinions of the person in question, and in this way be able to meet the individual openly and impartially and to respect the uniqueness of each person.

4. Pax benedictina - Benedictine peace

The ideal of the Benedictine personality is not the person who makes over and shakes up, not the person with an extraordinary religious endowment, not the great ascetic, not even the mystic, but that wise and mature person who understands how to create unity among people, who radiates an aura of peace and mutual understanding. This ideal image presupposes an important condition. I cannot simply decide to be a person who establishes peace. I have first to create peace within myself; I have to become reconciled with myself, with my weaknesses and faults, with his needs and desires, with my contradictory tendencies and aspirations. The creation of peace is not a program I can write on a banner, instead, it must proceed from an inner peace. And this inner peace is only attained by hard and consistent struggle for inner purity and by prayer in which I seek to accept everything that God sends in the way of my own or another's weakness.

Benedict requires of the abbot, above all, that he be able to establish peace. For that, the most important prerequisite is the ability to heal. Particularly in dealing with weak and sick brethren he must show himself a wise physician.

Thus Benedict writes:

> Let the abbot be most solicitous in his concern for delinquent brethren, for "it is not

the healthy but the sick who need a physician." And therefore he ought to use every means that a wise physician would use. Let him send *senpectae*, that is, brethren of mature years and wisdom, who may console the wavering brother and induce him to make humble satisfaction, comforting him so that he may not "be overwhelmed by excessive grief," but that, as the Apostle says, charity may be strengthened in him. And let everyone pray for him. For the abbot must have the utmost solicitude and exercise all prudence and diligence lest he lose any of the sheep entrusted to him. Let him know that what he has undertaken is the care of weak souls and not the tyranny over strong ones, and let him fear the prophet's warning through which God says, "What you saw to be fat you took to yourselves, and what was feeble you cast away." Let him rather imitate the loving example of the Good Shepherd who left the ninety-nine sheep in the mountains and went to look for the one sheep that had gone astray, one with whose weakness he had such compassion that he deigned to place it on his own sacred shoulders and thus carry it back to the flock. (R., 27).

We normally react to the weakness of others by irritation and anger. Weak and sick confreres hurt our sense of honor. We like to be proud of our group--the abbot of our monastery, the president of our corporation, the father of our family. If there are black sheep in the community, they are pushed to the outer circle where one hopes they will not be seen. Above all, outsiders are not to discover them, for they might harm the community's reputation. Sometimes we feel almost personally attacked and insulted if a member wanders off the beaten path. But Benedict orders the abbot to put aside all concerns with regard to the community's reputation and follow the individual in his weakness and confront it. In this way the abbot proves himself to be a true physician who allows himself to be wounded by the wounds of others in order to keep them in God's healing love. The most effective medicament in the abbot's pharmacopoeia is therefore prayer. When all human means, both loving consideration and severity, have proved ineffective, then "let him apply a still greater remedy, his own prayer and those of all the brethren, that the Lord, who can do all things, may restore health to the sick brother" (R., 28).

The ability to heal is a prerequisite if the abbot is to establish peace in the community. Peace cannot be dictated, cannot be brought about by discipline; it must grow out of a love that is strong enough to embrace all the faults of the members and heal them. Every superior of a community who constantly faces disagreements and conflicts knows that from experience. We are tempted either to crush conflicts and harshness, not allow them to surface, or we become resigned to them and take refuge in irony. In ourselves we construct a wall that separates us from the weak members and leaves us in our apparently healthy world.

The peace which the abbot is to establish in the community is neither a weak peace, nor a peace obtained by concessions, but a peace that does not shy away from the knife of separation. The abbot is not to suppress conflicts, but to face them openly. Thus Benedict has a special chapter concerning the correction and punishment of offending members. And the measures he therein prescribes strike us as drastic today. Benedict attacks the conflicts firmly, but not rigorously. His primary concern is the responsibility for the weak member and the desire to heal him.

For Benedict, peace comes into existence in a community by this process: the members expresses their own desires and needs and the abbot decides with the gift of discernment how far he should yield to the requests of individuals.

> Let us follow the Scripture, "Distribution was made to each according as anyone had need." By this we do not mean that personal preference should play a part, but consideration for infirmities. He who needs less should thank God and not be discontented; but he who needs more should be humbled by the thought of his infirmity rather than feeling important on account of the kindness shown him. Thus all the members will be at peace (R., 34).

These sentences contain an entire peace program. A pre-condition for the peace of a community consists in the members' ability to handle their own needs correctly. These needs may not be suppressed. On the other hand, they may not be justified by all sorts of reasons or even presented as demands. A need is always an admission of weakness. Still, a need has its right. And Benedict wishes that it be met. Always, however, with the admission: "I need this because I am too weak to deny myself." Because I have not made sufficient progress in self-control, I need good food for my spiritual balance. Because I still do not love God enough, I require strong human support for my psychological balance. If I thus admit my needs and confront them in the face of my weakness, then I am at peace with myself, and my needs do not become a threat to those who do not have them. Contrarily, those who have fewer needs, who perhaps get along with less-food, should not become proud and exalt themselves over others. That would only lead to fruitless self-comparison, which in the final analysis is the cause of all loss of peace. They should thank God that they need less. From this attitude, inner peace will be born. Gratefully fulfilling each other's needs and gratefully denying oneself-- we find the way to peace with ourselves and to peace within the community. Further, this attitude prevents murmuring which causes all spiritual progress to falter. Since murmuring threatens the peace of the community, Benedict inveighs against this vice:

> Above all, let not the evil of murmuring appear for any reason whatsoever in the least word or sign. If anyone is caught at it, let him be placed under very severe discipline (R., 34).

Murmuring indicates that I am not at peace with myself. But instead of acknowledging this condition, I blame the community, stirring dissatisfaction and confusion. I criticize everyone and everything; I always find the reasons for the disquieting conditions in others--the abbot, the members who do not abide by the Rule. I dare not to admit to myself that my judgmental attitude hides dissatisfaction within. And yet the desire to improve everything often proceeds from an unconscious rejection of myself. Because I cannot endure myself and my weaknesses, I refuse to support the weaknesses of others. Genuine improvement is possible only if it proceeds from love; that is, from the acceptance of one's own and others' weaknesses.

Present-day sociologists indicate a growing inability to maintain peace. Polarization of groups within society has increased. The parties have accustomed themselves to a more raucous tone of voice. They no longer look at others objectively or try to understand and take seriously their justified aims. The others are precipitately pictured as enemies to be combated. In this situation we might learn from Benedict how the peace process might be initiated.

In this matter Benedict does not set up a grandiose peace program, but he creates peace around himself. This method would also work for us. Every program has something combative about it. Today in the name of the good, in the name of positive ideals, programs are set up which initially are directed against something or someone. One fights for the Christian family and opposes all those that have uttered an opinion that contradicts our ideal. At great expense, propaganda is made on behalf of something positive. Benedict wants nothing to do with this kind of struggle. He does not set himself in opposition to someone or something but in favor of something, not of abstract ideals or programs, but of real persons, precisely, his small community of Monte Cassino.

In the midst of a world fallen into chaos, he builds up his community and strives to establish in it room for the peace of Christ. With all that, he does not assert the claim of exhibiting to the world a model of peace. Yet, without a claim to a mission, he brought Christian life to reality about him and labored day after day at the up-building of a Christian community of life. Walter Nigg calls Benedict "The building man," who, relentlessly and courageously, simply does the work at hand; a thoroughly positive man, to whom every negative tendency and every polemic was foreign.

To become a positive person who can build up without degrading others; therein lies one of the most important demands Benedict makes of us today. We should renounce promoting great programs. We may be tempted in the face of concrete and immediate matters to take refuge in programs. However it behooves us simply to carry out what we recognize as good and worthy of attainment, without constantly directing our activity against someone. Precisely in our de-christianized world we will achieve little if we constantly harp on its secularization. It is far more important for us to live our Christianity, without asserting that we are the only good people on earth. Benedict never utters a word of complaint about the apparently hopeless condition of the Church and the world of his time, but simply dedicates himself to his work. In his small community of monks he desires that peace become a reality. This peace did not affect the entire West immediately. But with his attempt to establish peace in his community, Benedict created a milieu which, down the line, produced its effects through the centuries and contributed essentially to peace in the West during the Middle Ages.

5. Stability and order

Historians emphasize that stability, the attachment to a specific community that Benedict demanded of his monks, served as a tranquilizer in the convulsive era of migration of nations. Of late, attempts have been made to play down the idea of stability. It is argued that in an age of mobility, stability is a relic of the past. But nowadays, a new understanding of the positive significance of stability is surfacing. Precisely in our mobile age when people are obliged repeatedly to change their place of abode and to accommodate themselves to new environments, stable points are a blessing. A monastery that has existed on the same spot for centuries is a guarantor of continuity. A monastery has roots in history and can therefore offer our rootless age consistency and security. From this continuity also arises a certain calmness with regard to daily events.

A community of persons who remain together all their lives can be a haven of security. One is sure to meet the same members who follow the same daily schedule. At a given hour they will sing Vespers. Simply knowing the rhythm of a community's routine permits participation in its life. One can depend on it and feel oneself sheltered in a community and its continuity.

Many young people have now come to realize how important it is to be able to lean on a solid community, how a permanent community can grant support and security. It means more than knowing several sympathetic members; it is a life carried on for generations, handed on from the old to the young, a community lasting through many days and through the years, in which so much has changed in individuals.

Nowadays, a growing aversion to commitment may be observed. People are afraid to commit themselves in marriage; they would like to try it first. People hesitate to decide on a profession; they prefer to leave their options open. And before they are aware of it, the doors slam shut. So people continue without decision and without firm commitment. Instead of the hoped-for free and enriched life, they garner rootlessness, vacillation and a fear of life.

Perhaps consideration of Benedict's stability can encourage many people to find themselves, to come to a decision and a commitment.

To preach that commitment is necessary for everyone does not help much. For in order to commit myself, I must experience sufficient strength and confidence. But possibly a community of committed men or women who have bound themselves together so closely that they can bear one another's weaknesses for a lifetime will encourage young people to come to a decision. Witnessing the blessings that determination and commitment have brought to others, can furnish the needed confidence to take the step oneself.

Stability, however, signifies much more than commitment and attachment to one place. For the early monastics, stability consisted essentially in standing fast when all sorts of thoughts and temptations threatened. Repeatedly, the hermits of the desert gave the advice to keep to one's cell and especially not to leave it when inner unrest and discontent were experienced. To remain in one's cell means not to avoid one's problems, but to confront them, not to run away from oneself, and not to take refuge in activities when it is necessary to come to terms with oneself. Stability as confrontation, as persistence in one's cell, would also in our day offer many a remedy for inner unrest. Pascal says somewhere that "all our unhappiness stems from one source, namely, that we are incapable of quietly remaining in our room" (Pensees, 139). If we would learn again to remain in our room, to persevere and to resist the temptation of constant change, then we might feel that many things within us become clear. We might get to the root of our problems and discover where our healing is to begin. Just as in the time of the migration of nations, when the Romans' only hope for balance was their cry for the games, so nowadays, Benedictine stability might have a healing effect on peoples' restlessness. Inner balance is not to be expected from external things, not from constant change, but only from a rediscovery of ourselves, from dwelling with ourselves, as Gregory so strikingly remarks regarding Benedict (Dial. 3).

A further element of Benedictine life is order--the schedule which gives the day a clear structure, assigning a suitable time for prayer and work, for silence and speech, for fraternal companionship and solitude. Frequently Benedict speaks of the suitable hour, the correct time. And he commands the abbot to be careful that everything is done at the proper time:

> The indicating of the hour of the Work of God by day and night shall devolve upon the abbot, either to give the signal himself or to assign this duty to such a careful brother that everything will take place at the proper hours (R., 47).

Everything has is proper time. The correct time for prayer is just as important as the correct time for work and the suitable period when the brethren can request something from the cellarer:

> The proper times should be observed in giving the things that have to be given and asking for the things that have to be asked for, that no one may be troubled or vexed in the house of God (R., 31).

Here Benedict clearly indicates why he so definitely divides the day and why he has all things happen at a suitable hour. The order of the day makes for peace in the community. It is not an order artificially imposed on a person, but offers the members the possibility of creating a certain order within themselves. Those who subject themselves to an external order experience that in this way they bring order into their whims and dispositions, set barriers to the inconstancy of their heart, and open a space in which the heart can become whole.

For Benedict the schedule underlines a healing factor. When a community gives itself a good timetable, that is a sign that it is healthy or can become healthy by following a good routine. In the Rule, Benedict regulates the life of the monastic exactly, because through this external and prudent regulation he wants to have the assurance that those who observe this order benefit from it interiorly and find healing.

A clear schedule makes a clear life possible. Many young people today have a new understanding of this fact. In their quest for an alternative life-style they set up their own rules in order to distinguish themselves from others in a purely external fashion. Their life-style becomes a symbol for them, signifying that they are different. They seek security in the regulations they establish for themselves. In the long run no one can exist without this inner point of reference, without the support of a protecting order. For if every day a person has to worry about the regulation of one's time, one expends one's energies needlessly. An order, once established and meaningful, frees a person to pursue what is essential; it supplies the necessary assurance in which one feels at home, not living comfortably, but seriously initiating the process of maturity.

While rejecting military drill and a purely external order of sterile principles whose *raison d'être* has long disappeared, some modern young people are beginning to have a new understanding of the healing power of order. They discover anew how much time is gained if the day is scheduled, if they do not simply act on feelings, but subject themselves and their feelings to a self-established order. Young people, in particular those who lean toward depression, experience that a schedule can be a support to which they can cling and thus rise again. For vacillating people, a firm routine can be better therapy than all psychological probing. Vacillation is not cured by theoretical insight, but by bringing order into internal chaos. As soon as life gains clear contours through external forms, it no longer sinks back constantly into the formlessness of human immaturity. Hence, it behooves us today to develop new methods, not sterile and impenetrable, but flexible and meaningful, for our personal as well as for our community life. We may either fashion our own forms or adopt those which tradition offers us. These latter have the advantage of having proved their worth through the centuries and shown themselves as salutary.

Not only has the meditation movement awakened a new understanding of forms, such as the gestures of the body, the correct manner of sitting and standing, but also the many attempts to living in community have uncovered how beneficial definite rituals can be for living together. If the day does not begin in a haphazard way, but with an established ritual--if all rise at the same time, begin the day with prayer in common, with a ritual greeting--then the day will not simply dissipate, but it will have a contour, a format, from which something can grow. To the forms we give to our life in common we may apply what Erhart Kästner says about the ceremonies of liturgy: "The soul feels comfortable in ceremonies. They are its dwelling place. Here it can be at home... The head wants novelties, but the heart always desires the same routine" (Die Stundentrommel, Frankfurt, 1978 p.77).

6. Benedict's understanding of community

Frequently in modern literature, we meet the human being as someone incapable of genuine conversation. One talks *past* others or engages in a monologue in the presence of others. One feels lonely, isolated, misunderstood. One has no community roots, but is "homeless," a stranger in a strange world. On the other hand, the youth of today is manifesting a profound longing for community. Activists among the young have given up trying to change society by great protest demonstrations. Nowadays, they want to create little worlds in which they can live as human beings. Everywhere communes arise in which people live together intensely, discuss their problems in common, mutually support one another and supply "the warmth of the nest." Money is shared, help is given to other members, attempts are made in common to help outsiders--especially marginal groups such as the handicapped, prisoners, drug addicts and migrant workers. As idealistic as many communes are in their goals, they nevertheless frequently fail. People feel overworked; tensions are unresolved. They want to solve all personal and interpersonal problems, and then discover that the more they seek to solve them, the more the problems multiply. Or the commune becomes a nest which indeed gives support, but into which many retire to escape the demands of life. The nest holds the individuals fast, does not permit them to grow and mature.

In this situation a consideration of Benedict's understanding of community might reveal some essential aspects for living in common. Benedict gives no theory of community life, only directives as to how people can live together--not only in the exaltation of a beautiful community experience, but in their daily routine as well. In Chapter 72, he lays down the conditions which make possible community life:

> Just as there is an evil zeal of bitterness which separates from God and leads to hell, so there is a good zeal which separates from vice and leads to God and to life everlasting.
> This zeal, therefore, the monks should practice with the most fervent love. Thus they should anticipate one another in honor, most patiently endure one another's infirmities--whether of body or of character--vie in paying obedience to one another with no one following what he considers useful for himself, but rather what benefits another. They should show tender pure charity to their brothers, fear God in love; love their abbot with a sincere and humble charity; prefer nothing whatever to Christ. And may he bring us all together to life everlasting!

The first requirement is reverence for others. In reverence I bow down before the mystery of the others. I contemplate it, but do not try to invade it. I also refuse to change others. With reverence, I believe that God himself loves them and will show each of them the best way.

Nowadays the desire to enter into the intimacy of another person on the pretext of helping him or her is almost epidemic. Without being aware of it, the "help" often consists in making the other person conform to my criteria, to my psychological principles, rather than really helping. With Benedict, reverence determines the manner of living together. This reverence ultimately rests on faith in Christ's presence in the brother or sister. Hence it is more than a human attitude; it has a religious coloring.

The second requirement flows from the attitude of reverence. It is mutual support. "Help carry one another's burdens" (Gal 6:2) is elevated to the basic law of community living. Each monastic is essentially a brother or sister to others, one who carries and supports them. One does not primarily want to change others, press them into a mold, but to support them. One is bonded to them, and precisely to their weaknesses. One bears with their bodily weaknesses--which he cannot change anyway--as well as with their weaknesses of character.

At present, many communities flounder because they insist too much on the mutual demand of change. Bearing with one another is an essential element of a genuine community. Naturally, this does not mean that one has to endure everything. In his penal chapters Benedict has shown that he knows how to confront problems--even radically, not only with words, but with decisive measures. But he also knows the limit where one can and should change another. Without the basic concept of mutual forbearance, a person always feels the compulsion of forcing change. For the other person always shows manners of acting and idiosyncrasies that irritate me.

Instead of wanting to get rid of everything that disturbs us in another, perhaps we ought to ask ourselves whether God does not want to commend the unpleasant brother to us, whether God does not wish to shake up our self-righteousness and self-assurance in order to open us to his love, which endures all things. The brethren are to obey one another and to consider what may benefit others. In a community we must listen to others, to their needs and desires, to their feelings and dispositions, to their ideas and initiatives.

By obedience, Benedict means that I assume responsibility for the community, that I allow myself to be affected by the needs of the community and try to do something about them, instead of insisting on my own needs and desires. My self-realization may not be put above that of the community. For only if I first open myself to it can I fully realize myself. An ideologue seeks self-realization which takes into account only one's own needs, and disregards the wishes of others. By service, by responsibility, by obedience, by openness toward others I find the way to myself.

Benedict describes the internal atmosphere of the community by the words, "They should tender the charity of brotherhood chastely." Fraternal love must be the hallmark of the community. This is a mature love, one not founded merely on feelings and emotions. By "chastely" Benedict means a love which has gone beyond the level from which I project my feelings onto someone else, consequently feeling myself bound to the other emotionally to such a degree that I become jealous of everyone who has good contacts with that person.

Benedict demands of monastics a love that does not exclude feelings, a love full of human warmth, but also a love which has matured, which probes deeper than mere feelings, which touches the soul of the brother or sisters and perceives the presence of Christ in the other. Such a love is more than feeling; it shows itself in concrete acts. Of this kind of love, Benedict says, in Chapter 35, that the brethren are to serve one another. And quite soberly he enumerates these services: in the kitchen, at table, in maintenance, in caring for the sick. Just as important as the atmosphere of mutual love, is concern that the routine services are carried out, that one is not distressed by the job of mopping up the floor, that discussion of the business of mopping does not take longer than the task itself. The fraternal love which should sustain a community must always be a practical love which is ready and willing to perform the most common daily services, to carry them out faithfully and without too much show of emotion.

A further element that Benedict envisions as the basis of his model community is love of Christ. This love must rank higher than all human feelings. Christ is the foundation of a community that can endure. Community means more than the beautiful experience of positive interpersonal relationships. If a community rests only on feelings, then either cliques arise, or disappointment and resignation, the result is because feelings alone do not do the "trick".

In his basic communities Jacques Loew has made an experience similar to that of Benedict:

> As is evident, the genuine fraternal community does not basically rest on feelings. Like the house built upon the rock, it rests solidly on Jesus and the word of God. Does that mean that feelings are excluded? Not at all. But feelings come later as a bud or a fruit on a tree. They are not the root of the tree. If we organize a team, a community, on the basis of joy ("to feel good with one another"), if in our discussions words like "to be understood", "in confidence", "granted", "I do not want to judge" occur too often, then the team will always be on an uncertain footing. This becomes a worry that engages us so much that one no longer has the time or the possibility to do anything else. If, on the other hand, the community bases itself on the desire to make Christ present and to act accordingly, then the rest will follow automatically (J. Loew, Ihr sollt meine Jünger sein, Freiburg, 1978, p.155).

Hence, it is an essential prerequisite for the permanence of a community such as a monastery, that it live by a goal outside itself, that it place Christ above itself. This protects the community from ideologies, such as those occasionally observed in communes nowadays. All the members of the community together serve Christ and consider him the center of their lives. For that reason a genuine human community, more permanent than feelings of trust and security, can develop around this focal point.

Benedict envisions a community of monastics. The word "monk" properly means "solitary." A monastic is one who lives alone, in solitude. Hence the community, as Benedict understands it, is always marked by a fruitful tension between solitude and life in common. Benedict's community is not a company of "bachelors" who do well by themselves, nor a nest of security for which many long today, but a mature community in which the individuals deliberately create their solitude and endure solitude before God. Community is not meant to rob one of solitude, but as a place in which the individuals very consciously seek solitude because they consider it a necessary element for human and religious growth. The community goes out of its way to make room for solitude and protects it for the individual.

A fundamental characteristic of solitude is silence, which Benedict regards as an essential element of the monastic life. In silence, the individuals free themselves from all ties to the world and to other people in order to stand before God. For the early monastic silence was a sign of our pilgrimage, a sign that we have here no lasting city in which to dwell. In silence we withdraw from the world, become estranged from it in order to learn that our true homeland is heaven. In and through his monastic community Benedict creates a place of silence in common, a place in which togetherness is repeatedly interrupted in order to view God whom every individual must face. Community is not a bonding together, but an aid for individuals in their solitude to dare to appear before God in order to adhere, not to any human being, but to God.

CONCLUSION

Fifteen centuries have passed since Benedict's day. But a glance at his Rule has shown that Benedict transcends this difference in time with a message that can show us a time-proven way to God and the way for the healing of human beings. We need only listen patiently as Benedict announces it to his community in the Prologue of his Rule:

> Listen, my son, to your master's precepts, and incline the ear of your heart. Receive willingly and carry out effectively, your loving father's advice, that by the labor of obedience you may return to him from whom you had departed by the sloth of disobedience (Prol.)

We honor Benedict best if, instead of honoring his person and heaping encomiums upon him, we open ourselves to his message. As long as we tarry with the person of Benedict, we run the risk of projecting our own ideal image into it. For the dates of Benedict's life are so uncertain that they can easily tempt us to fill the *lacunae* with our imaginary pictures. But Benedict's Rule stands before us solid and foursquare. It makes a demand to which we must take a stand. If we listen to it, then we act according to the mind of Benedict, who never wanted to preach himself but only Christ, to whom he has shown a practicable way by his Rule.

ABBREVIATIONS

Dial - Life and Miracles of St. Benedict (Book Two of the Dialogues) by Pope St. Gregory the Great. Translated by Odo J. Zimmerman O.S.B. and Benedict R. Avery, O.S.B., The Liturgical Press, Collegeville, MN.

BOOK II

THE LEGACY OF ST. BENEDICT

Philip and Sally Scharper

The Legacy of St. Benedict was produced and copyrighted by The National Broadcasting Company, Inc. in 1980 in association with the U.S. Catholic Conference. BMH Publication was granted the right to print the transcript in conjunction with the booklet *Benedict of Norcia*.

© BMH Publications
Schuyler, NE 68661

THE LEGACY OF ST. BENEDICT

The way of life he established nearly fifteen hundred years ago has outlasted empires and apart from the Church itself is the oldest living force in Western civilization.

For many, Rome was still the center and support of the known world when young Benedict came there as a student toward the beginning of the sixth Century. Christianity, after centuries of persecution, had now become the official religion of the Empire, with Rome as its center. But the once-proud city still bore the scars of earlier barbarian invasions and when Benedict walked its streets, the grandeur that was Rome was almost more a memory than a reality.

The physical decline was mirrored in its morals as well. Rome had become almost a symbol of cruelty, lust and greed. The Church itself was marred by dissension, and Christians often fought each other in the streets. Dismayed and disgusted by what he saw about him, the young Benedict broke off his studies and left Rome to search for God in solitude.

Every great religion has numbered those who sought the absolute in solitude--in Christianity the first towering figure was John the Baptist. Following his example, thousands of men and women in the early Christian centuries went out into the rocky deserts of Palestine, Egypt and Turkey. They left highly sophisticated cities, even as Benedict left Rome, because, in the words of Thomas Merton, "the solitary life is an arid, rugged purification of the heart."

SUBIACO:

For Benedict, that "purification of the heart" took place in a cave at Subiaco, some thirty miles from Rome. For three years he dwelt alone, "seen only by the eyes of God," in the phrase of his first biographer, Gregory the Great. Later ages, in their devotion to Benedict, have adorned the site with art and architecture, almost obscuring the fact that this was a cave, giving little shelter from winter's frost or summer's heat. This cave became the place wherein God shaped the spirit of the young hermit through long days and nights of prayer and austerity.

Then God called him from the solitary life to serve others. First, nearby shepherds whom he instructed in the faith; then, a growing number of disciples who wished to share his way of life. That first small community gathered around Benedict in work and prayer could not guess the mark it would leave upon history as monasteries grew in size and number. In the darkness of a barbaric age, monasteries preserved the treasures of classical literature and were the only schools available to princes and peasants alike. Subiaco was the mustard seed of the Gospel parable.

MONTE CASSINO:

Benedict next founded a monastery on Monte Cassino, halfway between Rome and Naples. Ironically, Benedict's house of peace has been repeatedly destroyed by war--the last time by allied bombers in World War II. Funds for its reconstruction came from every part of the free world--for Monte Cassino is sacred not in Italy alone, but in every nation to which the followers of Benedict first preached the mystery of the Cross.

As in the cave at Subiaco, centuries of devotion have ornamented the simple cell of Benedict. Here he prayed, studied and wrote until his death toward the middle of the Sixth Century. His ornate tomb seems almost inappropriate for a man who insisted on simplicity in all things, whose life was a single-minded search for God. The monastery he founded here was like the Scriptural city built upon the mountain, which cannot be hidden.

For almost fifteen centuries, Monte Cassino has been looked upon as the cradle of monasticism in the West, and Benedict himself the Patriarch for the thousands of men and women who have followed his way of life. Among the first and greatest of these was his twin sister, Scholastica, joined to him in death as in life. The inscription reads in part: "This single tomb holds them both--

born together and in their lives one in holiness." Scholastica's love for her brother and his love for her set them apart from the practice of the desert monks and the teaching of many Hindu and Buddhist masters, who insisted that even family affection must be, not purified, but purged away. Benedict chose an opposite path and in his Rule made the family a model of what a monastery should be.

RULE OF ST. BENEDICT:

This basic respect for the truly human characterizes the entire Rule of Benedict, a short, simple document which set forth his ideal of the monastic, indeed, the Christian life. On almost every page we see Benedict himself, an extraordinary man who combined a sweeping vision with a keen eye for detail. It was a document destined to strengthen the Church and change the course of Western civilization.

ST. GREGORY:

Benedict had written a spiritual guide for his followers. The man who saw its value for the world was Gregory the Great, Benedict's first and most influential biographer. Gregory gave up wealth and political power to become a monk and then was elected

Pope. As wave after wave of barbarians swept over what was left of Roman civilization, the Church could become either a fortress under siege or could move out to conquer its conquerors. Gregory chose to conquer and in one of his many bold, brilliant moves he summoned from his own monastery a monk named Augustine and sent him forth to England. The Anglo-Saxons were famous for their cruelty, and Augustine was as reluctant to be a missionary as Gregory was to be Pope.

LINDISFARNE:

So successful was Augustine's mission that he has long been called the Apostle of the English. But the task of converting the British tribes did not fall upon Augustine and his companions alone. A band of Irish monks established a monastery here at Lindisfarne. From this tiny island they gradually established a network of monasteries across the north of England, and the Church grew strong. But the monks had no defense against the Danish Vikings. Their repeated raids finally forced the monks to flee, and Lindisfarne lay abandoned through the course of two centuries with only the sound of the wind and wave heard through its ruins.

It was finally built as a Benedictine monastery after the Norman Conquest, with the Celtic cross a reminder of the Irish origin of Lindisfarne, the "holy island." The monks had come to preach Christ to a rude and warlike people, but they surrounded that Christ with the beauty of art and architecture which glow more brightly against the darkness of the age in which they were produced. The works which survive reveal artists patiently but passionately dedicated to their tasks.

It would be almost impossible, for example, to calculate how many hours were required to produce such a masterpiece as the Lindisfarne Gospels. The manuscript blends into harmony strands of Celtic, Anglo-Saxon, and Byzantine culture, and the portraits of the Evangelists are stylized in a manner not unlike that of modern art. As Benedictine monks and nuns spread over Europe, they carried with them these arts of calligraphy and illumination. Monasteries and convents required books because Benedict's Rule called for stated hours of private spiritual reading every day. But the Benedictine copyists also painfully reproduced the works of classical Roman writers, and without their efforts much of Latin literature might have simply disappeared.

Sheep thus became an important part of most monasteries. Their wool supplied cloth for the monk's habits, but their skins, which could have been used for other purposes, provided the parchment on which manuscripts were copied, and every manuscript represented a capital investment. To copy one work of Cicero, for example, would require a team of scribes and a flock of sheep.

JARROW:

In the north of England, that investment would have to be made again and again. Marauding Vikings would plunder or destroy whatever the monks could not carry with them as they fled, including their precious books. When the invaders had gone, the monks would return. Work would resume in the ravaged fields, and the copyists would again bend over their books.

These Anglo-Saxon monks were merely carrying on the tradition of Monte Cassino, for the Rule of Benedict saw neither contradiction nor compromise in bringing together the love of learning and the search for God.

Less than a century after Augustine had come to England, Anglo-Saxon monks would themselves become missionaries to northern Europe. Sons and grandsons of pagans, they communicated a deeply personal faith, and a reverence for beauty. Shortly after the church at Jarrow was dedicated, plague killed all the monks except the Abbot and a young novice named Bede.

Bede spent all his life in the monastery at Jarrow. He wrote on every subject he knew, the Scriptures, the Church Fathers, Latin literature, mathematics, astronomy, and his *Ecclesiastical History of the English People* made him the most famous scholar in Europe. When he grew too old to write, he dictated to a young scribe, even on the very day of his death.

RIEVAULX:

Bede left a detailed description of life in his own monastery, and it was much the same as life in Benedict's Monte Cassino, or in hundreds of monasteries which grew up through the Middle Ages. It was the pattern of life here at Rievaulx in England. Even from its ruins we can draw some image of what a monastery was like in the centuries before the Protestant Reformation. There was the Chapter House--so named because each day a chapter of Benedict's Rule was read to the assembled monks. These daily meetings were presided over by the Abbot, who was elected from the community by the community. Abbot means "father," and he was expected to be both the spiritual director of his monastic family and administrator of its affairs. Yet on important decisions he was required to seek advice from all of his monks, including the youngest.

But in time the spiritual beauty and strength of many monasteries became more apparent than real. The lands they had reclaimed and built upon now yielded considerable income. The rich and powerful were often their patrons, and pious pilgrims left gold and jewels in gratitude. Sometimes, as here at Rievaulx, more were admitted to the monastic life than were suited to it, and lack of discipline threatened its stability.

The world outside the monasteries had itself grown spiritually cold. Tudor England had entered a selfish, grasping age. On December 3, 1538 Henry VIII ordered the suppression of most monasteries and convents. He confiscated their lands and wealth which he tossed into eager hands of his courtiers. Some 800 monastic families were dissolved. What Augustine had begun almost a thousand years before now lay in ruins, and a way of life older than England's monarchy had drawn to a close, seemingly forever.

WESTMINSTER ABBEY:

The ancient and honored Benedictine abbey, Westminster, now passed into possession of the King. The tradition of Benedict had been fed, as from a silent spring, by British monks and nuns who found in the cloister that peace which surpasses understanding. Now harsh laws were enacted against them, and Parliament declared the King "Supreme Head of the Church of England."

There were no longer monks to begin their day in the Chapter House with a reading from the Rule, or a discussion with the Abbot of some decision facing the monastery. The Chapter House was used now to store the government's financial records. The glory of the British monasticism never fully faded. In 1607 the last surviving monk of Westminster founded three monasteries and a convent in France and Flanders. English men and women chose exile to join these communities, hoping for the time when they could return to their native land.

AMPLEFORTH ABBEY:

The time would be 1802--the place Ampleforth, Yorkshire. The new monastery followed the pattern of Bede's Jarrow and Benedict's Monte Cassino. There were fields for farming--Benedict wished every monastery to supply its own needs. A school and college were established, now among the most prestigious in England.

The chants no longer heard within Westminster now filled the Church at Ampleforth. The Benedictines had returned from exile. The poet Petrarch had called the cave at Subiaco "the threshold of Paradise," and the Benedictine tradition had always seen the monastery in the peace and charity of its members, a remembrance of that Paradise in which God placed Adam.

The tree of life in the monastic paradise is the cross, and to be a monk is to embrace the Cross "sharing in Christ's sufferings," wrote Benedict, "so that we may share in His Kingdom."

STANBROOK ABBEY:

For Benedictine nuns in England "to share in Christ's sufferings" was more than a phrase. Henry's Act of Suppression had driven them from their convents, adrift in a hostile world. Deprived by law of the right to follow a vocation in their homeland, generations of women had gone abroad to France to enter a British Benedictine convent founded there in the reign of Queen Elizabeth. They were imprisoned in the French Revolution, then, destitute and uncertain of their future, returned to England in 1795 and established the first Benedictine convent since the days of Henry VIII.

Stanbrook Abbey thus became a living link with a long and often splendid history, for Nuns had been part of the Benedictine tradition from its birth. Bede, in his history of the Anglo-Saxon Church, wrote tributes to two Abbesses, Hilda and Ebba, who held jurisdiction over houses of both monks and nuns. In the early Middle Ages, an Abbess was sometimes as powerful as an Abbot or a Bishop, and nuns were among the scholars and writers of a period noted for its creativity.

The Benedictine nuns and monks follow the same Rule and at its heart is prayer in common throughout each day. This Liturgy of the Hours, readings from the Scriptures and sacred song, Benedict called "Opus Dei" (the work of God) and nothing, he warned, was to be placed before it. This Liturgy binds the community together and shows its unity with Christ, present, both in the Eucharist, and in God's Sacred Word.

For Benedictines, this cycle of the liturgy, the work of God, moves in an unending round of worship from hour to hour, season to season, year to year. Together with the Eucharist it is the sourcespring of their lives. Along with prayer, Benedict stressed the virtue of work. "Ora et labora"--"worship and work"--alternate in the daily rhythm of Benedictine life.

Yet, in that tradition, work has occupied a rather curious place. Curious, at least, to many of us, whose ideas of work are drawn from an industrialized, competitive society. Work can become a necessary evil, and many people are bored or unhappy with what they do. Benedictines are encouraged to develop their talents through a work they like, so long as it does not interfere with their principal goal: to search for God within a community in which all share that search.

If Benedict is The *Father of Europe* it is because the work of his sons and daughters nurtured and preserved Western civilization. Artists, woodworkers, architects, masons, scholars and farmers have, over the centuries, found that to work is also to pray. In 1440 the invention of movable type made the production of books faster and inexpensive. Presses turned out more books in two decades than all the volumes copied by all the scribes in the previous centuries. Catholic bishops lauded the new process as a "divine art," but did not seize upon its advantages. The Benedictines did--the first press in Italy was at Subiaco. A print shop was established here at Stanbrook over a hundred years ago and is the oldest private press in England. Its first book, not surprisingly, was *The Rule of Benedict.*

In that Rule, when treating of manual work, Benedict upset the values of the Roman world, and our own. Any work is honorable if it truly serves the need of others. "Blue collar" or "White collar" may be a significant distinction in society--it has no meaning in a Benedictine community. The only question asked of a nun or a monk is not, what work you do? but, is it done to the best of your ability?

METTEN:

The very years which saw the return of Benedictines to England also saw their expulsion from Bavaria in southern Germany. The monastery at Metten, long famed for its baroque art, library and illuminated manuscripts, was suppressed by Napoleon in his sweep through Europe. Fifteen years after Waterloo the Benedictines returned to resume their quiet life of teaching and learning, but the world was to change for the monks at Metten.

They were to hear the cry of their people: "How can we sing the songs of the Lord in a strange land?" German Catholic immigrants to America needed priests who understood their tradition and language. Their ancient faith was dying, would it be restored to life? In 1846 nineteen men left Metten for America.

ST. VINCENT ARCHABBEY:

The ancient faith would be strengthened; and through these men, the fourteen hundred years of Benedictine tradition would be brought to the New World. From their first monastery, St. Vincent's near Pittsburgh, would come, within a century, ten abbeys spread from Florida through America's heartland to Alaska. The man who, all unknowing, carried the seeds of that future in his hands was Boniface Wimmer, called to the frontiers of America by the pleas of his countrymen.

Log cabin and frame structures were slowly replaced by buildings which the monks constructed from bricks they had made themselves. The forest was cleared, crops sown and harvested amid the daily round of prayer and study. A typical Benedictine monastery had risen in the wilderness. The old buildings erected by the pioneer monks blend almost symbolically with the new. The cells of American monks bear no resemblance to those of either Metten or Monte Cassino, and even Benedict might have been surprised at the number living in a single monastery and the variety of their works. But the strength of Benedict's Rule is precisely that it allows for change yet preserves a unity amid variety.

Boniface Wimmer died before the church was even begun. The altar stands in strong contrast to the crude altar where he first celebrated Mass in the wilderness. But no matter. A Mass may be more solemn, but no more sacred, when celebrated on a marble altar than upon a battered table in a concentration camp, so long as those who gather round it recognize the altar for what it is. The Hebrew word for altar means both the place for ritual sacrifice and the table for a meal. For Christians, the altar is the sacred place whereon Christ renews the Sacrifice of the Cross and becomes the Bread of Life.

When Boniface Wimmer brought Benedictine men and women to America, the Rule of Benedict was submitted to a new test. Could the latter be adapted to the raw frontiers of a young nation largely anti-Catholic, and yet retain the spirit which had given it life for fourteen centuries? History has given the answer. Adjustments were made, where necessary, to a sprawling country, largely immigrant and rural; but the spirit burned, if anything, more brightly than in Europe.

An Abbot was still spiritual father of the monastic family, and the Rule remained his guide, and theirs. Good zeal, for Benedict, meant carrying out, in detail, one of Christ's most difficult injunctions: "Love one another, as I have loved you." Monks are to be brothers: bearing patiently one another's infirmities and irritating characteristics. Putting other's needs before their own. In short, they are to form a family where young and old grow together, under the same discipline, gathered around the same altar, sharing the same food. In the words of an ancient hymn, "where there is charity and love, there is God."

Even on the frontier, Benedictines carried on their tradition of learning as part of their search for God. Within five years of his arrival, Boniface Wimmer's backwoods' library contained, in addition to works of philosophy and theology, Greek and Roman classics, and a collection of rare books and manuscripts. Today the monks of St. Vincent's are scholars, writers and preachers who staff a coed college and conduct a major seminary.

SISTERS OF PERPETUAL ADORATION ST. LOUIS:

There is one spirit but many gifts, and Benedict's Rule allows freedom for every gift. The Sisters of Perpetual Adoration in St. Louis are contemplatives. "Music," said John Paul II, "exalts what is human and enriches what is religious and divine."

The Church's sacred music has always centered on the Eucharist because the Eucharist is the center of the Church's life. At the altar, heaven and earth, the Old Testament and the New, God and His human family, Christ and His Mystical Body, are brought together in a mystery which causes even our greatest poets to stammer and our finest theologians to fall into silence. The realities of the Eucharist are too many and too rich for the mind to grasp or the tongue to utter, only the loving heart begins to understand the transformation when a community enters into the Passion, Death, and Resurrection of Christ.

Only the eyes of faith can see Christ living in the consecrated bread and wine, and living in the needs of others. For He is neither divided, nor divisible. The Christ Who says, "I am the Bread of Life," will also say, "I was hungry, did you give me to eat?"

The Eucharist means not only receiving but giving. The Christian's "Amen" at Communion acknowledges that they recognize through faith the undivided Christ, and commit themselves to *be* Eucharist--bread broken and wine poured out to sustain others. These nuns have grown old being Eucharist. And being old, they are the objects of special attention. Benedict in his Rule, states that gentle consideration must always be given to the aging.

The old and the sick, vulnerable members in any society, occupy a place of honor and reverence in the world of Benedict, because others must see Christ in their weakness and pain. A society can be judged by how it treats its vulnerable. Our society tends to shunt aside the elderly. They are deemed no longer useful, and not to be useful is almost to be a non-person. Here, every effort is made to insure that these are, in fact, the golden years. The elderly remain within their Benedictine family, and contribute to it wisdom and serenity--and they continue to contribute to the work of the family.

Here at St. Louis, much of that work is devoted to sending aid to more than 200 Benedictine convents and monasteries in Asia, Africa and Latin America, the so-called mission lands. The United States itself was a mission country until this century, depending on Europe for many of its priests and nuns, who were dependent in turn on Europe for much of their material needs until their small, struggling communities could become self-sufficient. And now it has become America's time to support the young churches in the Third World.

To provide the vestments, medicines, books and other needs the nuns depend on the generosity and prayers of lay people. The mail room thus becomes an important link in a chain of compassion spanning four continents. The cries of the poor are heard and answered.

When Benedict insisted that the model for the communities following his Rule was the family, it was not merely a useful metaphor. He meant it. And Benedictine fun is family fun--which does not require gadgets--just one another. When some people hear that a young woman has entered the convent, they say with a shudder, "she has gone to her grave." This would seem to be a rather lively graveyard.

The family prayer of the Benedictine community and private prayer are alternating rhythms in the daily life of a nun or monk. The first word of the Rule is *ausculta*-- "listen," part of prayer is listening. "Ora et labora"--"to pray and work," prayer must also have hands.

ST. JOHN'S, MINNESOTA:

St. John's in Minnesota is a large Benedictine monastery of about 230 monks. "Jesus saw them following and said, "What do you seek?" They answered, 'Teacher, where do you live?' He replied, 'Come and see.' So they went and saw where Jesus lived, and they stayed with Him." Those first disciples who heard these words were rather ordinary people, only the call was extraordinary.

Many ordinary men and women in America have heard that call and have followed Christ as Benedictines. To that ancient tradition they have added an American virtue: a willingness to experiment, to try the new.

When this Abbey Church was dedicated in 1961, its architecture was considered revolutionary and many old monks shook their heads in sorrow. Now it attracts more visitors than any other edifice in Minnesota, with the exception of the State Capitol. The Church and other modern buildings at St. John's are symbolic. The monks here are of a new breed: sons and grandsons of immigrants, they are *American* Benedictines.

The multi-colored facade window was designed to suggest the splendor of the liturgical year but its restless energy also reflects a typically American blending of old and new which characterizes St. John's. Its Institute for Ecumenical and Cultural Research is unique in the world. St. John's pioneered Public Radio Broadcasting in Minnesota.

Microfilm Library:

Advanced technology is used by the Hill Monastic Manuscript Library to preserve precious documents and manuscripts on microfilm. It is a revolution in scholarship, making it possible to consult previously scattered sources of cultural and social history. Here over 72,000 ancient manuscripts have been recorded, the total collections of 200 libraries in twenty countries. It took a scribe four or five months to painfully produce a text of 200 pages. This microfilm process reproduces such a text in minutes.

Liturgical Press:

The Manuscript Library preserves for scholars treasures of the past. The Liturgical Press makes that past live for the people of God today. Since 1926 the Press has published books, magazines, pamphlets, and official Sacramentaries and Lectionaries which have enabled generations of American Catholics to find their source of life in Liturgy and Scriptures.

Workshop:

From the carpenter shop at Nazareth to that of St. John's is a journey of 2000 years, and a short step. The example of Joseph and the tradition of Benedict stress the spiritual value and dignity of labor. The Benedictine motto of "Worship and Work" shows the link between liturgy and labor. To pray with the hands is as honorable as the work of scholarship or teaching. All that matters is that one try to pray well. In an era of planned obsolescence and shoddy workmanship, where things fall apart before the final payment, the monks seem to "pray well."

Benedict stressed manual work for economic as well as spiritual reasons; he wanted his monasteries to be self-supporting. Using wood from their own forests, the monks have made sturdy modern furniture for the college dormitories, the monastery and guest rooms, and the office of the Abbot.

Library:

Modern furniture, architecture, technology demonstrate that typical Benedictine flexibility at which the Americans have shown themselves so adept. But in education particularly, as Benedictines they must challenge certain features of American colleges and universities, which too often issue diplomas as passports to professions and careers. Benedictines hope to send out not replaceable cogs in the big machine, but creative non-conformists.

College of St. Benedict:

The College of St. Benedict, five miles from St. John's, is adjacent to St. Benedict's Convent of Benedictine women monastics. The first Benedictine women came from Germany to teach the children of immigrants. Within a generation they had established twenty schools in the Dakotas and Minnesota, and founded hospitals and orphanages in territory stretching from the Mississippi to the Pacific. "O Pioneers, 0 Pioneers" exulted Walt Whitman, and Benedictine women were among them.

Benedicta Arts Center:

Outreach to the larger community around it also characterizes the Benedicta Arts Center. Academically it offers superb training in visual arts, music, theater and dance for the students of St. Benedict's and St. John's. But it is also a cultural center for the surrounding towns and villages, and serves the cultural needs and interests of a quarter-million people. They may, of course, find themselves at an artistic frontier: the work of an award-winning Benedictine woman.

Concerts and recitals by students and faculty alternate with performances by nationally famous orchestras and ensembles in this acoustically perfect auditorium. During the academic year the *Benedicta Arts Center* sponsors many professional, college, and community events, which annually attract large audiences from the colleges and surrounding communities.

The Arts Center aims to encourage the students' own creative powers, and develop the artists and audiences of tomorrow. When Abbot Boniface Wimmer was sending Benedictine men and women to found schools on the raw American frontier, he said: "A Benedictine school which does not give just as much attention to art as to knowledge and religion is a very imperfect one." In that sense, St. Benedict's and St. John's are traditionally Benedictine: "celebrating Christianity through music, art, and drama."

Updated and revised by Fr. Jonathan R. Licari, O.S.B.

SAINT MEINRAD ARCHABBEY

Monks from the renowned Swiss abbey of Maria-Einsiedeln founded Saint Meinrad in 1854. Abbot Henry of Einsiedeln sent two monks in answer to a request from Father Joseph Kundek who ministered to the German population in southern Indiana. The purpose of the foundation was to work with the German community and to found a seminary. The monks attended to these goals soon after their arrival.

Pastoral assistance began at once. In 1857 the school was opened and in 1861 a complete seminary program was inaugurated. More than 10,000 students have been educated at Saint Meinrad. Of these, about 3,100 have been ordained priests. In 1867 a small press was begun which today has developed into the flourishing Abbey Press and related ministries.

Saint Meinrad has made the following monastic foundations: New Subiaco, Arkansas (1878); Saint Joseph, Covington, Louisiana (1890); Marmion, Aurora, Illinois (1933); Blue Cloud, South Dakota (1950); and Prince of Peace, Oceanside, California (1958).

The community today (1992) numbers 140 monks. The majority live and work in the monastery or in apostolates connected with the monastery such as the press, the seminary schools, the retreat house, the offices, and the shops of the institution. A number of young monks is generally away at universities both here and abroad pursuing degrees to return as teachers. The monastery is responsible for the care of seven parishes and several chaplaincies.

While the task of every Benedictine monastery is to live the Holy Rule, the translation of this document is shaped by the tradition of the house, the leadership of its abbots and the make-up of the monks. Saint Meinrad has traditionally shown a loving care for the public worship of the Church. The arts have been cultivated and the rich holdings of the library--more than 150,000 volumes--contribute to a life of scholarship.

During the past decade, large building projects have been successfully completed. The monks have guided to completion the construction of a new monastery, a new library and the renovation of the former monastery for use by the seminary schools. Active planning projects an optimistic future.
Updated and revised by Fr. Leo Ryska, O.S.B.

ST. BENEDICT'S PREP, NEWARK:

In Newark, New Jersey an Abbey almost as old as St. Meinrad's also continues to prepare young men for the future but there is a difference. When the white middle-class fled to the suburbs in the 1960s, the monks had to decide whether to close their prep school or stay. They stayed.

Benedictines have always been educators of the young and have taught them to sing. But "liturgical singing," warned Benedict, "is not authentic unless the mind is in harmony with the voice."

As different ethnic groups began to dominate the population of inner city, many wondered if St. Benedict's could continue its proud tradition of college preparatory education. The monks met the challenge with energy and imagination. The school had served well the children of upwardly mobile middle-class Germans, Irish and Italians. It continues its tradition although the student body has changed. There are other changes as well. Half of the students are non-Catholic and some white parents are beginning to send their sons in from the suburbs to insure they get a good education with the right kind of companions.

Each school day begins with a reading from Scripture and the singing of several hymns. It almost seems like a prep school version of the "opus Dei"--the community worship of the monks in the abbey next door. But the idea came from the students, not the monks. The "opus Dei" is followed by a brief talk by the Headmaster, who is also the wrestling coach.

The irritating questions of "why can't Johnny read, or spell, or write" are never asked by the parents of these students. St. Benedict's is also the only school in New Jersey to belong to a network of thirty schools in the United States, Canada, and the Virgin Islands. These schools exchange students on a voluntary basis for two-month courses with no charge for tuition, room, or board. Over 90% of St. Benedict's students go on to college, including some of the most prestigious.

ERIE, PENNSYLVANIA:

In downtown Erie, Pennsylvania, Benedictine nuns carry on another tradition--feeding the poor. The decay of American cities has become so pervasive that it has been termed "urban blight" and like most diseases in our society its principal victims are the poor, and they call for a special response from Benedictines. In his Rule Benedict states that the poor who come to the monastery should be welcomed with even greater care than other guests, because in them "Christ is more truly received." In his biography of Benedict, Gregory the Great writes that rather than turn the poor away, Benedict would give them whatever he could find in the monastery, even though there should be nothing left for the community. No need to worry how the rich will be received: Benedict remarks perceptively, that "the very fear one has of the rich procures them honor." In its treatment of the poor, as on almost every other point, the Rule is rooted in the Scriptures: both enjoin a sense of solidarity with the poor, the outcasts. It was with these Christ ate and drank. Approximately one person of every six in the United States is poor by the Government's own standards, and two-thirds of the world's peoples are locked in dehumanizing poverty. Here the Benedictine tradition is not enough. Charity is needed, but justice is demanded. The nuns who run this soup kitchen also run an Office for Justice and Peace and are thus linked with every major community of religious men and women in the country who have defined action toward justice as their major ministry.

HOSPITAL:

In dealing with the sick, Benedict's Rule makes a startling statement. "Before all things and above all things care is to be taken of the sick, so they may be served in very deed as Christ Himself." He seems to place it almost on the same level as community worship, which must take precedence over every other activity of the monastery.

Ours is an age of medical marvels and human creativity reflecting the Divine Creator when technology is turned to the support of life. Yet the complaint is often made in our society that the healing arts are becoming merely the healing profession--that doctors and nurses can seem almost as cold and impersonal as the machines they operate.

For a nun to be a highly-trained medical technician is, fortunately, not new. What is new is for a nun to be an ecumenical chaplain in a public hospital. A nun is no longer routinely assigned to an apostolic work, after consulting her prioress, she is often free to choose a ministry in which the needs of others are met by her talents.

It takes special talents to meet the needs of special people, patience, of course, and respect if one cannot summon up love and compassion. Respect for the handicapped seems to be draining from our society. Too many are bundled off to overcrowded hospitals and homes and out-of-sight does become out-of-mind. These nuns, unlike Christ, cannot cure with a touch. They can only smile encouragement and, above all, listen, in the deep sense of Benedict's Rule: to "listen with the ear of one's heart"--"heart" means the depths of one's person.

The monk and nun are thus to "listen" to the Rule, the Abbot to "listen" even to the young monks. Every one has important things to say, if they know someone else will be "listening."

The Benedictine life is a counter-culture in our society. Vows of poverty, chastity and obedience are scandal enough. They also vow *stability*: to remain for life a member of the monastic family they have entered, and *conversion*: constant unflinching self-examination and discipline.

It has always been easy either to romanticize or ridicule the life of a Benedictine monk or nun. We envy the tranquil beauty of so many monastic settings where they can live alone with God--"the world forgetting, by the world forgot." Or we can dismiss them as cold, selfish ascetics who have 'fled the world' from either fear or mistrust. In either case, their cross seems of their own choosing, and rarely one of heavy, rough-hewn timbers.

The word "monk" can mean "solitary" but also single-minded seeker of God in the company of others who share that quest and forge a unity of minds and hearts. No matter where lived out, it is a desert journey but the desert is not the absence of others, it is the presence of God. For those with eyes to see and ears to hear God is present in all things. The bell becomes His voice which summons one to worship or to work.

WESTON PRIORY:

Weston Priory is set amid the Green Mountains of Vermont, and the monks here do what Benedictine monks seem to have been doing since Augustine and his monks made clearings in the forests of England, and Boniface in Germany felled trees to build those monasteries around which hundreds of towns and cities would grow. There are obvious differences. The job was a bit harder for Augustine and Boniface. The monks of Weston seem to hope that by their witness, they can help to bring the liberating Gospel of Jesus to their North American society and culture once again. For this is an essential dimension of the monastic movement: monks have been challenged to be prophets, their calling reaching back to that time when John the Baptist came out of the desert to proclaim that the ax must be laid to the root of the tree.

Quite consciously, the Weston monastic community seems always aware of the continuity between the Hebrew Scriptures and the Gospel, between Israel and that renewal movement which came to be called Church. Weston Priory was founded by a monk from Jerusalem, in the land which the three great Abrahamic faiths call "holy." That monk, Leo Rudloff, instilled in the new-born community the vision--and *task*--which inspired his own view of the monastic movement: "Remain open to the Holy Spirit." Inspired by John the Baptist, whose name means "God is gracious," the monastic community, he said, should be a leaven *in* the world, in the midst of the society, as an "embassy of the Reign of God," as a sign of the human search for the God who is seeking us. And like an earlier Jerusalem monk, St. Jerome, they should see no contradiction in the vocation *both* to seek God in the wilderness and to proclaim God's justice and peace in the cities. Fed by this prophetic monastic inspiration, the monks of Weston have, at times, left the remoteness of their monastery to protest injustice in Appalachia, to call for non-violence and nuclear disarmament at the United Nations and in Washington; to stand in solidarity with the suffering poor in the *barrios* of Mexico and Nicaragua, and in the inner-cities of Hartford and Brooklyn. And the world's cries of pain have found a hearing *within* the monastery. The ancient tradition of monastic hospitality has taken on new form as the Weston brothers declared their monastery a Sanctuary--a "sacred space," a "safe place"-- for the protection of refugees fleeing the violence of Central America.

But these are not "monks on the march," as one headline put it. They are a close knit, creative, prayerful community, which looks on each brother as a gift. In their daily work, as in the whole of their life, the brothers encourage one another to develop those gifts which are both expressive of their persons and serving the common good. Caring for the woodland, apple orchards, and garden reflects the community's environmental concern. Brothers also share together in woodworking, musical composition, hospitality, and the graphic arts; and they assume equally the responsibilities of their common life. They seek to be a community of learners, of equal disciples, practicing the "search for God" in the world of *today,* listening for God's Voice as it can be heard most clearly--in the poor, the suffering, the outcast. And they invite others to join them in their learning, their listening: together with a congregation of Benedictine Sisters in Mexico, the Weston monks sponsor a retreat center in Cuernavaca, Mexico, to enable other North Americans to be touched directly by the lives of the poorest.

Music holds a special place in this community. Expressing the prayer, experience, and values of the whole community, the composition, production, and distribution of the brothers' songs is the gift and work of all. Through this common work, the brothers' music has become a part of the lives and prayer of people throughout the world.

But it is the gift of *community* which roots and calls forth this life of prayer, work, hospitality, and outreach: the fundamental choice to offer oneself to one's brothers in joyful service, in a common vision and hope, and in an abiding faithfulness. It is the gift of Emmanuel, God-with-us, just as it was for the desert people of ancient Israel, who also danced in simple rhythm around an altar or a campfire. "The Word became flesh and dwelt among us... The reign of God is in your midst." It is the hidden Presence gathering the world into unity that is the foundation of the monastic life, of all human life. We too may hope to see it, because a young man 1500 years ago, amid the mountains of Subiaco and Monte Cassino, embraced a search for God that brought him to community. It became for Benedict "the only journey worth taking." In the joy of that

journey is the unmistakable sign of the presence of God.
Updated: Bro. Philip Fronckiewicz, O.S.B.

THE MISSIONARY BENEDICTINES OF ST. OTTILIEN

While the Bavarian and Swiss Benedictines set their sights on the New World, serving the immigrants as pastors and teachers, a new branch of the Benedictine family, the Missionary Benedictines of St. Ottilien, was born, setting its sights on the Third World with the sole aim of grass-root evangelization. Within a very short time this new Missionary Benedictine Congregation of St. Ottilien has grown to be the third largest Congregation (Province) within the Benedictine order. Its members of 1097 (1991) monks and 1270 (1991) sisters of the Missionary Benedictine Sisters of Tutzing are, today, found on all Continents.

The Benedictine Congregation of St. Ottilien owes its origin to Andreas Amrhein (1844-1927), who entered the Abbey of Beuron (Germany) in 1870 in the hope of combining a Benedictine monastic lifestyle with an active mission apostolate. It was at a time when several Benedictine monasteries in Germany were again re-opening after they had been closed down by government decrees in 1803 in the wake of the so-called secularization. Most of these communities tried to reorganize monastic life along strictly contemplative lines which virtually excluded the possibility of monks doing missionary work. And yet, there was a tremendous revival of the mission spirit in the Catholic Church all over Europe. It brought about the establishment of mission societies and Congregations whose members committed themselves exclusively to the spreading of the Gospel.

Amrhein, recalling the role Benedictine monks played towards the evangelization and civilization of Europe in the middle ages, was adamant that the sons of St. Benedict were once more called to take "the gospel and Christian civilization" to countries and continents where Christianity was unknown. When he realized that he would never be able to do this as a monk of Beuron, he put himself--with permission of his abbot--under the authority of the *Prapaganda Fide* in Rome. The prefect of the Propaganda supported his ideas and made it possible for him to start a mission house in Southern Bavaria. The mission house gradually developed into a Benedictine monastery and became an abbey in its own right in 1902. By 1914, three more abbeys were established and the Benedictine Missionaries of St. Ottilien were recognized as an independent Congregation within the Benedictine family. The Abbey of St. Ottilien was raised to the rank of an archabbey. Since then the Archabbot of St.

Ottilien is at the same time president of the Congregation.

The first group of missionaries left St. Ottilien for Africa already in 1887. They fulfilled their call to the missions under great difficulties. The monks built a monastery in Pugu (Tanzania), but within a year it was destroyed by rebels who rose up against the German colonial rule in East Africa. Several Benedictines were killed. Physical exhaustion and the murderous climate took a heavy toll. No fewer than 80 missionaries were sent to East Africa between 1887 and 1895 (10 priests, 31 brothers, 39 sisters). By 1895 twenty-one of them had succumbed to tropical diseases. In spite of this, the Benedictines continued their mission in East Africa and laid the groundwork for the Catholic Church. Two archdioceses and eight dioceses have developed in the area originally entrusted to the Benedictines of St. Ottilien. The Congregation of St. Ottilien has two abbeys (Peramiho and Ndanda) and one conventual priory (Hanga) in southern Tanzania, giving evidence of a strong Benedictine presence in that part of Africa. The three monasteries have a combined membership of 316 (1990), 165 of whom are local monks.

Although the Benedictines of St. Ottilien regarded their mission work in East Africa as top priority, they accepted other mission fields in the course of the years and undertook foundations in a number of countries. In 1909, they followed a call to East Asia, establishing abbeys in Tokwon (North Korea) and in Yenki (Manchuria) and building up the Church in an area that included North Korea and the eastern part of Manchuria. Both abbeys were suppressed when a communist regime came to power after the Second World War. A number of monks were killed or died in a Korean concentration camp. The survivors started a new monastery in Waegwan, South Korea. The Abbey of Waegwan has today (1991) 136 monks, among them 120 Koreans.

In 1921 the Propaganda Fide entrusted the Missionary Benedictines of St. Ottilien with a new mission field in Zululand (South Africa). It became a diocese in 1951, headed by a local bishop since 1975. One of the former mission stations, Inkamana, developed into a Benedictine monastery and was raised to the rank of an abbey in 1982. Ten years later, it had 34 expatriate and 14 local monks.

After the First World War, it became obvious for the Congregation that it had to reach out beyond Germany (where it had three abbeys) in order to broaden and consolidate its basis of the many mission endeavors it was embarking on. Foundations were made in Switzerland (Uznach 1919), in Venezuela (Caracas 1923), Colombia (El Rosal 1961) and in the USA (Newton, NJ in 1924). All of them have meanwhile developed into abbeys. Another foundation in the USA, the Benedictine Mission House, was founded in 1935 and became one of the most important mission procures of the Congregation. Many of the mission projects undertaken by the Benedictines of St. Ottilien in Africa and Asia, would be impossible without the support of the monks of Schuyler, Nebraska.

As the mission churches in Africa and Asia gradually developed into local autonomous churches with the local clergy taking over the responsibility from the expatriate missionary monks, the Missionary Benedictines of St. Ottilien made all the more effort to implant the Benedictine way of life in former mission countries. It resulted in the establishment of conventual priories in Hanga (Tanzania) and Nairobi (Kenya) and of new foundations in the Philippines, in Uganda and Zambia.

The mission apostolate of the Benedictines reached a new dimension when the Council of the Congregation of St. Ottilien began to sponsor efforts of local men who tried to build up monastic communities in Africa and Asia. The Congregation offers to help them with the formation of candidates and to give other assistance when this is requested. Such help is given without imposing on these communities structures and traditions that are alien to them. On the contrary, they are encouraged to live out the Benedictine ideals in a way that leaves room for the incorporation of genuine local customs. This support program, which was started in 1988, is being tried out by different groups of young men in Togo, Zaire and India. Such communities, seeking affiliation with the Benedictine missionaries of St. Ottilien, are given the opportunity of being fully integrated into the Congregation.

In 1992 the Benedictine Congregation of St. Ottilien had 14 abbeys, 2 coventual priories, and a number of religious houses and pre-foundations in 16 different countries.

Fr. Godfrey Sieber, O.S.B.

Additional books in the
SCHUYLER SPIRITUAL SERIES

Grün/Scharper
Vol. 01 **Benedict of Norcia**
The Legacy of St. Benedict
(1992) 108 pages $ 3.95

Ruppert/Grün
Vol. 02 **Christ in the Brother**
According to the Rule of St. Benedict
(1992) 61 pages $ 3.60

Clifford Stevens
Vol. 03 **Intimacy with God**
Notes on the vocation to celibacy
(1992) 120 pages $ 3.95

Clifford Stevens
Vol. 04 **The Noblest Love**
The Sacramentality of Sex in Marriage
(1992) 82 pages $ 3.70

Books in preparation:

Grün	**The Challenge of Midlife**
Grün	**Dreams on the Spiritual Journey**
Grün	**The Mass and Spiritual Maturity**
Colombas	**Dialogue between God and Man**
Grün	**Health as a Spiritual Task**
Krepphold	**The Sermon on the Mount**
Grün	**Unmarried for the sake of God**
Doppelfeld	**Encounter with Christ Vol. 1 + 2**
Grün	**The Challenge of Silence**
Grün	**Prayer and Selfknowledge**
Grün	**Fasting**

AND OTHERS